Busy Brains for Girls:
Supporting Executive Functioning and Neurodiversity in the Classroom

Written and Illustrated by Tenille Dowe

Copyright © 2025 Tenille Dowe

All rights reserved. No part of this book may be reproduced in any manner whatsoever without prior written permission of the publisher.

First Printing, 2025

Published by Creative Heart Connection
www.creativeheartconnection.com

ISBN 978-1-7636536-9-6

Busy Brains

Supporting Executive Functioning and Neurodiversity in the Classroom

For Girls

Written and Illustrated by Tenille Dowe

Her bedroom is a sanctuary
where she can explore.
Free from the chaos of school,
it's a place to restore.

Her special interests bloom without any rush.
In a world where her family
knows what she likes so much.

With love and comfort,
anxiety and overwhelm is chased away.
A predictable haven where she feels okay.

In a bustling corridor where she roams,
feeling anxious because she's not at home.

The noise and crowd are quite a fright,
turning her world into a dizzying and overwhelming plight.

With compassion, support and a few things done differently,
things will feel better and right.

In a busy classroom it's often too loud,
noise-cancelling headphones feel like a cloud.

Sensory overload can be tough,
where every sound seems to be just too much.

Headphones can help in creating calm,
a quiet space, allowing her to focus on her own.

It's not just about silence, it's about finding peace,
helping her manage when
sensory challenges increase.

So, when the world feels too noisy and bright,
these headphones can make things feel just right.

In the quiet of the morning while
others are on the playground,
she finds her way.

Arriving at class before the bustling fray.
With the corridor empty,
she feels at ease,
far from the noisy and crowding students,
her mind is at peace.

When she enters the classroom, her bag spills wide,
amidst the chaos and increasing anxiety.
She doesn't know where to start inside.

Though papers and books may scatter and stray,
she needs a schedule to find her way.

Her world appears unorganised and cluttered.

Order brings peace,
and with a clear plan,
her worries release.

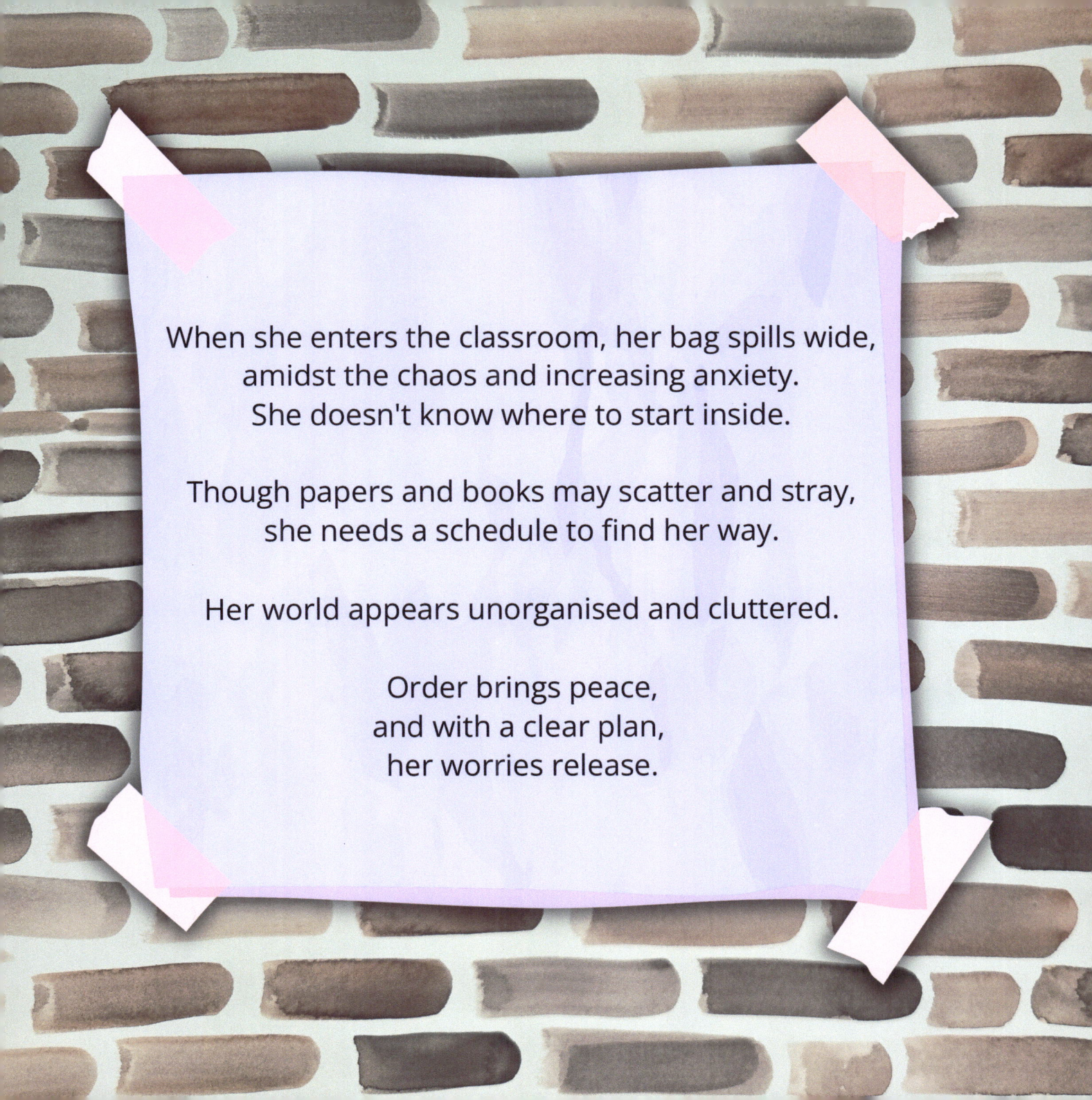

In the classroom, success began
when the rules and routine were clear.

For her, organisation brought
a lightness and cheer.

With a tidy desk, focus would flow,
and learning became easier,
allowing her to grow.

In this structured space,
she found her stride.
Thriving with confidence, side by side.

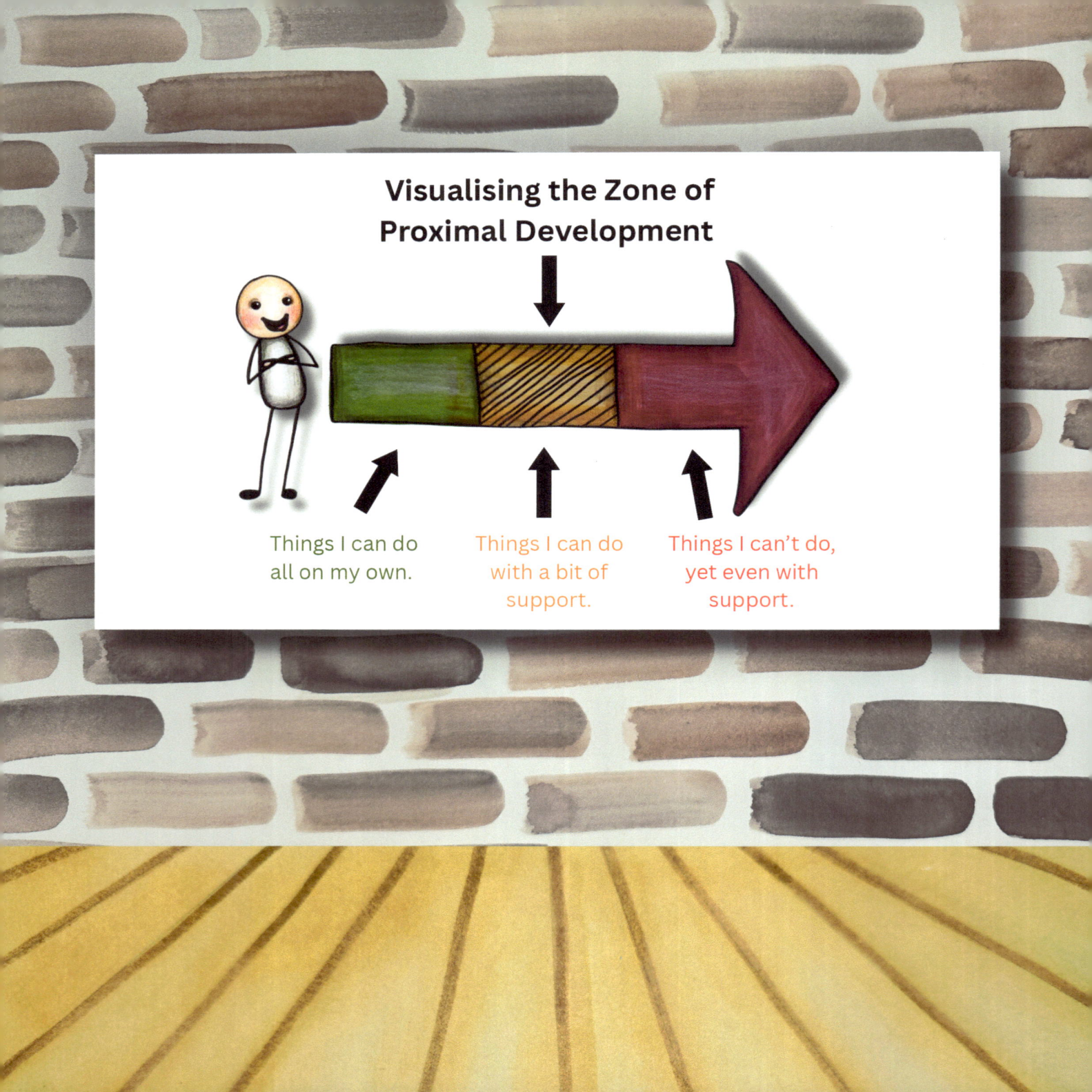

In the Zone of Proximal Development,
she'll find a space where learning can be fun
and her mind can unwind.

With a little help, new skills she can gain,
just like riding a bike, or catching a train.

It's where she will be challenged, but not alone.
With guidance and support,
her confidence in learning can be grown!

In her class, a traffic light system is the key.
Where students use colours to set their
learning free.

Red means you're stuck,
even with help you can't proceed.

Yellow is just right,
where a little support is all you'll need.

Green shines bright for tasks you can do
without help and at great speed.

A visual timetable helps her see,
what each day holds,
so she can be anxiety-free.

It brings a rhythm, a calming delight.
Creating consistency,
making everything right.

With each task shown,
she knows what's in store.

Reducing worries and opening the door,
to a peaceful mind,
where chaos no longer reigns.
In this structured dance,
only clarity remains.

Interoception is the sense that lets you see,
when you're hungry,
thirsty, or need to pee!

It helps you know when you need a break,
like when your tummy rumbles,
or your brain feels like it might ache.

At school, it guides you,
keeping your needs in sight.

Showing when to pause
and make things right!

In the classroom's bustling pace,
she sometimes feels out of place.

Interoception shouts,
her heart is beating so fast,
as if it was in a frantic race.

Struggling with the task at hand,
frustration starts to show.

Overwhelmed by the feeling of failure,
her patience runs low.

In her mind, she searches for calm,
hoping the chaos will go.

In the classroom, when she can't start a task,
she feels stuck and trapped.
Her head lowers, she curls up in a tight ball,
all her options seem sapped.

Eyes closed, tuning into her inner state,
sensing and feeling her own heartbeat
as her thoughts circulate.

During the hardest lesson,
she wishes for a way to feel less
confused and dazed.

In the classroom, when things start to feel tight,
she remembers the system:
Green, yellow and red light.

Yellow means she needs help,
so in future she will raise her hand high.

She still needs reminders from the teacher,
no need to be shy.

With the traffic light system in mind,
she can start to feel safe.
She can ask for help,
her learning can take flight.

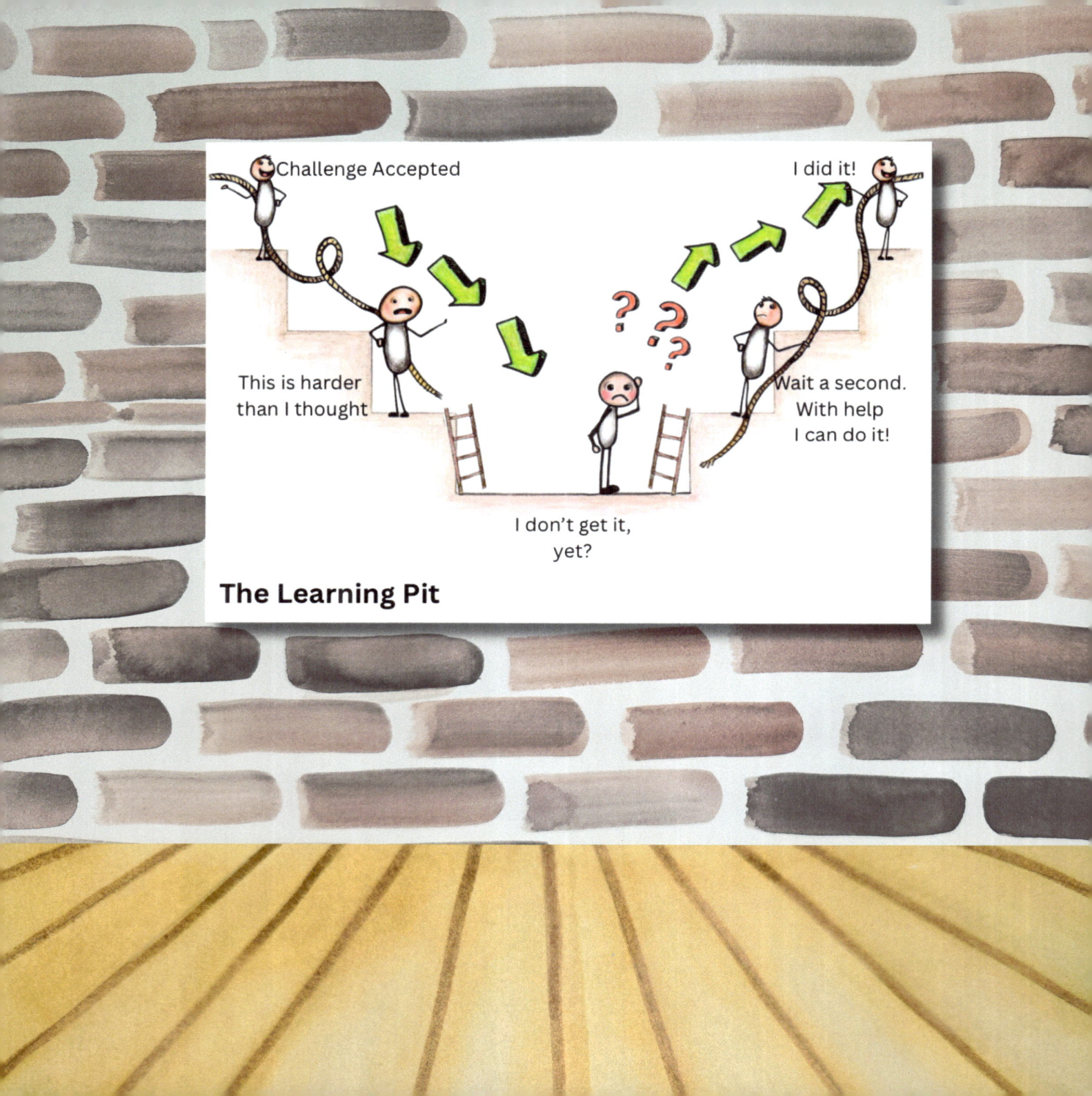

Her teacher calmly told her a story.....

"Imagine you're on an adventure,
deep in the Learning Pit.
Where challenges are hard, but you don't quit.
You take a leap, though the climb seemed steep,
and found it tougher than you did at first peep.

With your teacher's help, you made a start,
using a checklist, you play your part.

Step by step, you work with zest,
and now you're moving towards doing your best.
Keep going, you're on the right track,
with effort and grit, there's no turning back".

Deep in the Learning Pit,
she took a daring leap.

Accepting the challenge
that seemed rather steep.
She found it harder than she initially thought,
but her teacher's support was kindly sought.

With a checklist in hand,
she began to progress,
steadily working her way towards success.

You took a daring leap into the Learning Pit,
facing challenges that seemed quite steep.

With your teacher's support,
a checklist in hand,
you found your way.

Growing stronger with each passing day.
You conquered the pit
with a triumphant cheer.

Your success is well-earned,
that's perfectly clear!

At school and in the classroom,
she finds her stride with supports
that are just right.

Adjusting to challenges,
she's ready to take flight.

A calming corner awaits
when she needs to refocus her mind.
Helping her regroup, leaving worries behind.

With these adjustments in place,
her potential's truly unconfined.

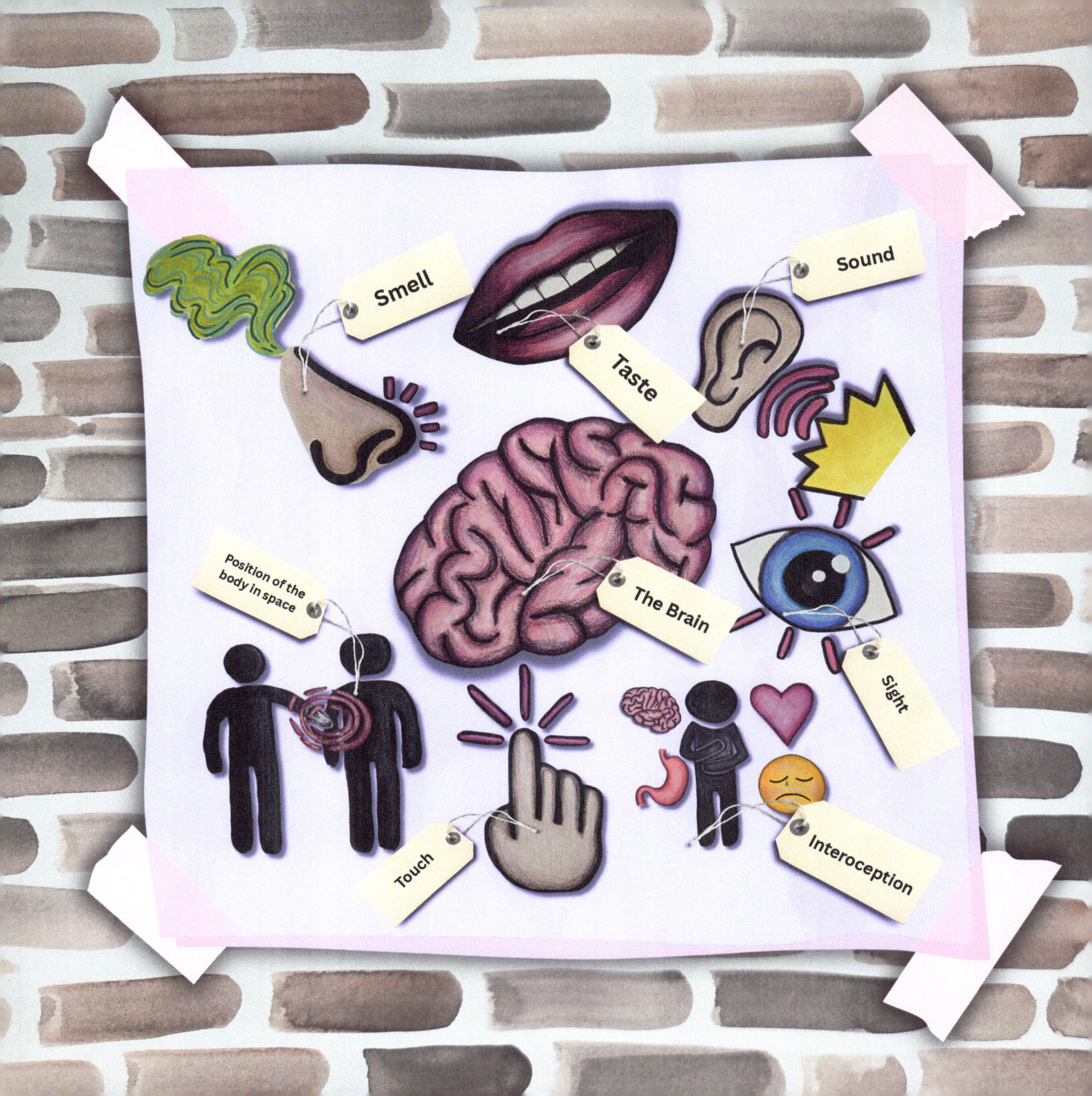

www.ingramcontent.com/pod-product-compliance
Lightning Source LLC
Chambersburg PA
CBHW041110070526
44583CB00003B/128